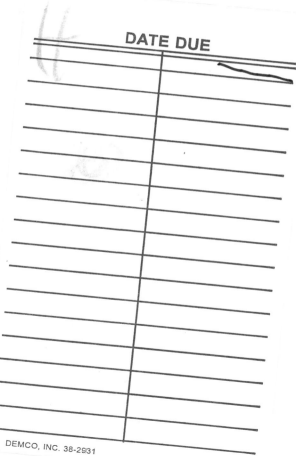

DATE DUE

Life in a Pond

By Allan Fowler

Consultants

Robert L. Hillerich, Professor Emeritus,
Bowling Green State University, Bowling Green, Ohio;
Consultant, Pinellas County Schools, Florida

Lynne Kepler, Educational Consultant

Fay Robinson, Child Development Specialist

CP Children's Press®
A Division of Grolier Publishing
New York   London   Hong Kong   Sydney
Danbury, Connecticut

Project Editor: Downing Publishing Services
Designer: Herman Adler Design Group
Photo Researcher: Feldman & Associates, Inc.

Library of Congress Cataloging-in-Publication Data

Fowler, Allan.
    Life in a pond / by Allan Fowler.
      p. cm. – (Rookie read-about science)
    Includes index.
    Summary: Introduces the animal and plant life in and around ponds.
    ISBN 0-516-06053-8
    1. Pond ecology—Juvenile literature. 2. Ponds—Juvenile literature.
[1. Pond ecology. 2. Ponds.] I. Title. II. Series.
QH541.5.P63F68   1996
57405'26322–dc20   95-39661
                                          CIP
                                          AC

This is a lake. It's big and
it's deep.

This is a pond. It's small and it's shallow.

Sunlight reaches the bottom of a pond. This allows plants to take root and grow there, all across the pond.

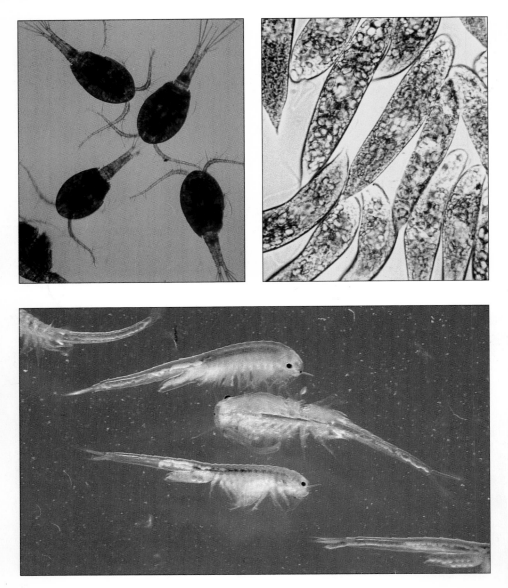

6

A pond is a wonderful
place to learn about nature.

You can see all kinds of
life in and around a pond.

The smallest pond life
is plankton — very tiny
plants and animals floating
in the water.

Plant plankton, or algae, sometimes forms a green film on the surface of a pond.

Plankton is food for some of the pond's animals.

And they, in turn, may be eaten by larger animals.

9

Bass, sunfish, and perch
are some of the fish you
might find in a pond.

You might also find shrimp
or crayfish or clams.

Turtles and frogs and
snakes and snails often
live in or around ponds.

Big dragonflies may fly
over the pond.

Other insects, such as
water striders, walk on
top of the water.

Ducks, geese, and swans
visit ponds to rest, and to
feed on floating duckweed.

Long-legged birds such as egrets and herons may wade through a pond.

Deer, moose, raccoons, and other mammals come there for water and food.

17

One animal, the beaver,
makes its own ponds.

Beavers live in underwater
homes called lodges.

The beavers cut down
trees with their sharp teeth.
Then they use the trees and
mud to make a dam across
a stream.

A deep pond forms behind
the dam — deep enough
so the beavers can build
their homes!

Trees, such as willows
and cypresses, often
grow around ponds.

Some kinds of plants float in pond water. Water lilies, like these, can cover a pond with their flat leaves. They often have pretty flowers.

Plants that take root
along the shores of a pond
include cattails and other
reeds, tall grasses, ferns,
and pondweeds.

Waste material from dead plants and animals sinks to the bottom of a pond. As the waste builds up, the pond becomes more shallow.

Now the plant life on its shores can grow closer to the center of the pond.

After many years, reeds and grasses may grow all across the pond. The pond has become a marsh. Or it may even dry up completely.

But new ponds are
always forming.

Some are made by
nature, some by people —
and some by beavers.

29

Words You Know

lake

pond

marsh

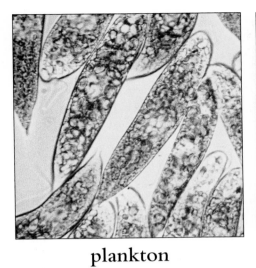

plankton

algae

dragonfly

water lilies

Index

About the Author

Allan Fowler is a free-lance writer with a background in advertising. Born in New York, he lives in Chicago now and enjoys traveling.

Photo Credits

Tony Stone Images, Inc. — ©Gay Bumgarner, cover
SuperStock International, Inc. — 22; ©Steve Vidler, 3, 30 (top left); ©Neal & Molly Jansen, 15
Photri, Inc. — 5, 30 (top right); ©Betts Anderson Bailly, 23, 31 (bottom right)
Visuals Unlimited — ©CABISCO, 6 (top left); ©T.E. Adams, 6 (top right), 31 (top left); ©John Sohlden, 25
Root Resources — ©Anthony Mercieca, 6 (bottom); ©Don & Pat Valenti, 9, 31 (top right); ©Kohout Productions, 21
Animals Animals — ©Colin Milkins, 10; ©Kathie Atkinson, Oxford Scientific Films, 11; ©E.R. Degginger, 12; ©Mark Stouffer, 13, 31 (bottom left); ©G.I. Bernard, 14; ©Leonard Lee Rue, 18; ©Perry Slocum, 19
H. Armstrong Roberts — ©D. & P. Valenti, 16; ©T. Ulrich, 17
Valan Photos — ©Dennis W. Schmitt, 20
Earth Scenes — ©John Stern, 24; ©Zig Leszcaynski, 26; ©Michael P. Gadomski, 27, 30 (bottom)
©Cameramann International, Ltd. — 29
COVER: Mallard duck in pond near pink water lily